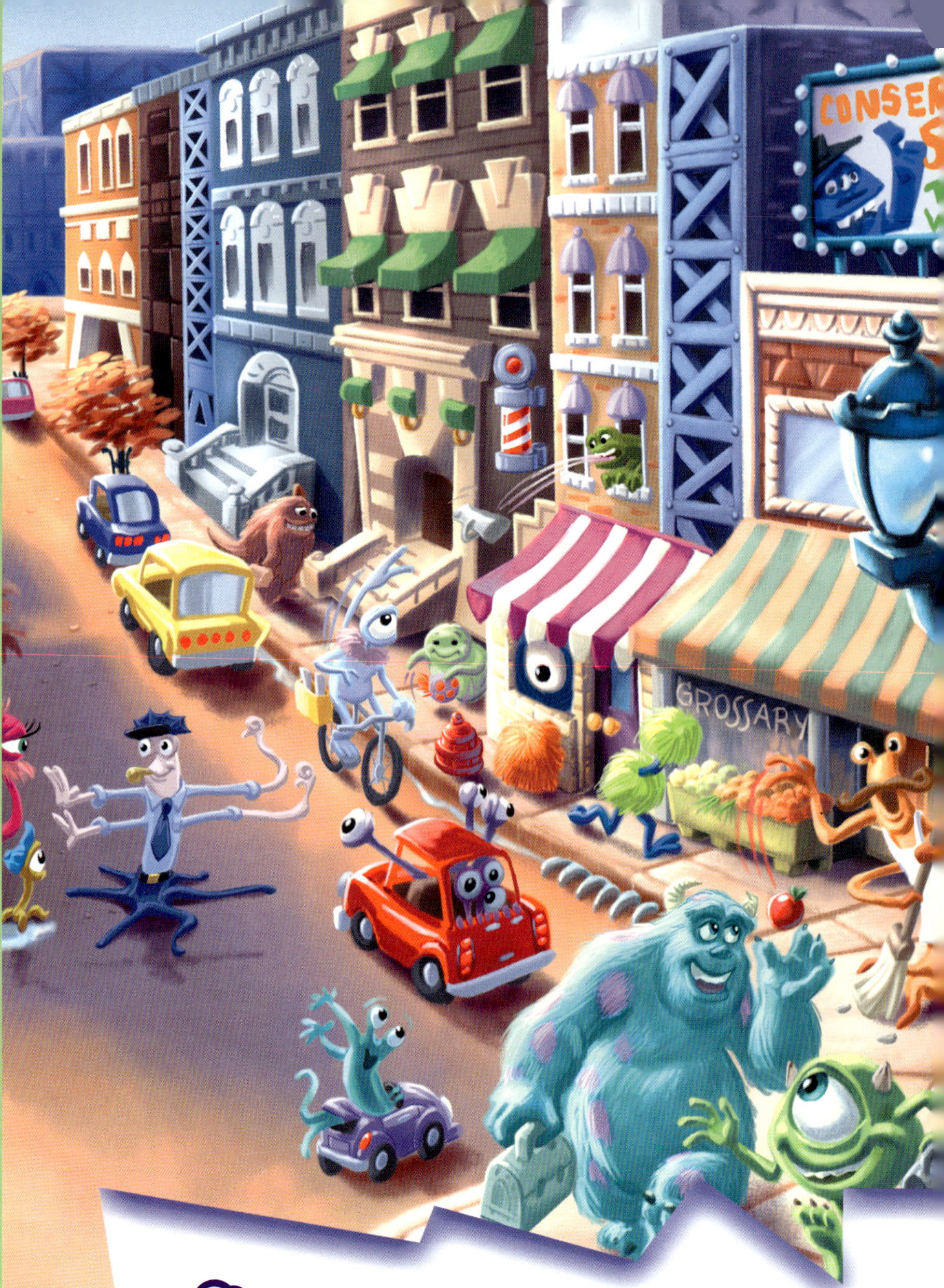

Sulley was a monster who worked for Monsters, Inc.

Scarer

Very hairy.
Very scary.
Children were **wary**.

He and his best friend Mike
— what a team! —
they made kids scream.

Then there was Randall . . . angry Randall, **jealous** Randall, **invisible** Randall.

Randall wanted to be Scarer of the Month just like Sulley.
But Sulley was the best.

GAME

← LEFT — RIGHT →

  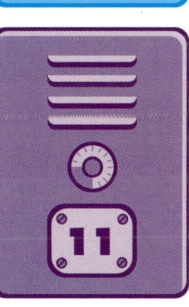 

 Trainee   Scarer

Monsters scared children while they waited to fall asleep. It might seem mean, but it made them scream.

This powered the cars and warmed the houses and lit the lights in the city of Monstropolis.

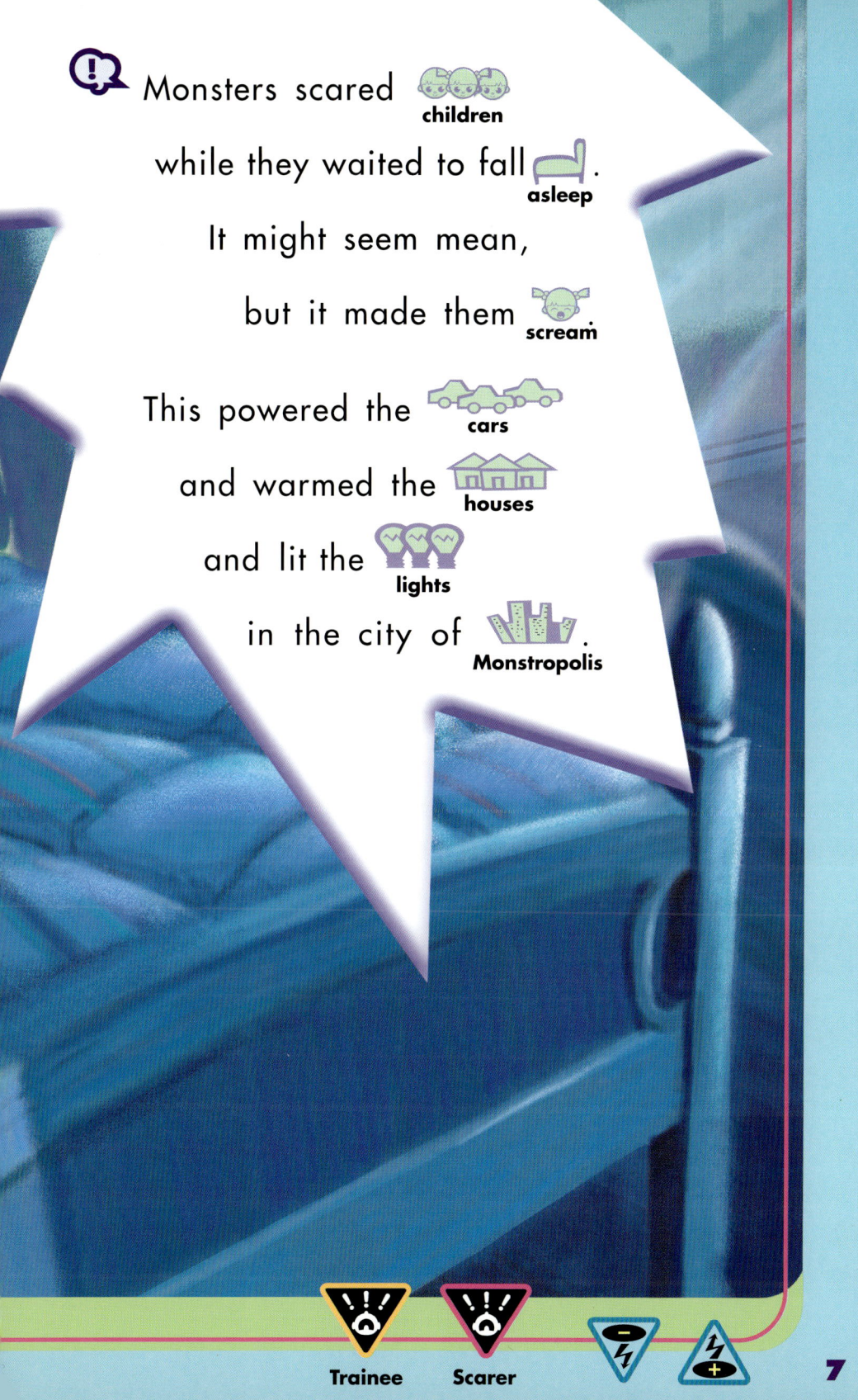

Monsters thought children were **poison**;
all of you girls and boys
and even your toys.

Until one day a child went **astray** and **grabbed** Sulley's tail when he looked away! A little girl came through the **closet** door and shouted:

"Kitty!"

GAME

Trainee  Scarer

Sulley didn't know what to do. So he hid the little girl in a bag and went to find Mike, who was at a **restaurant**.

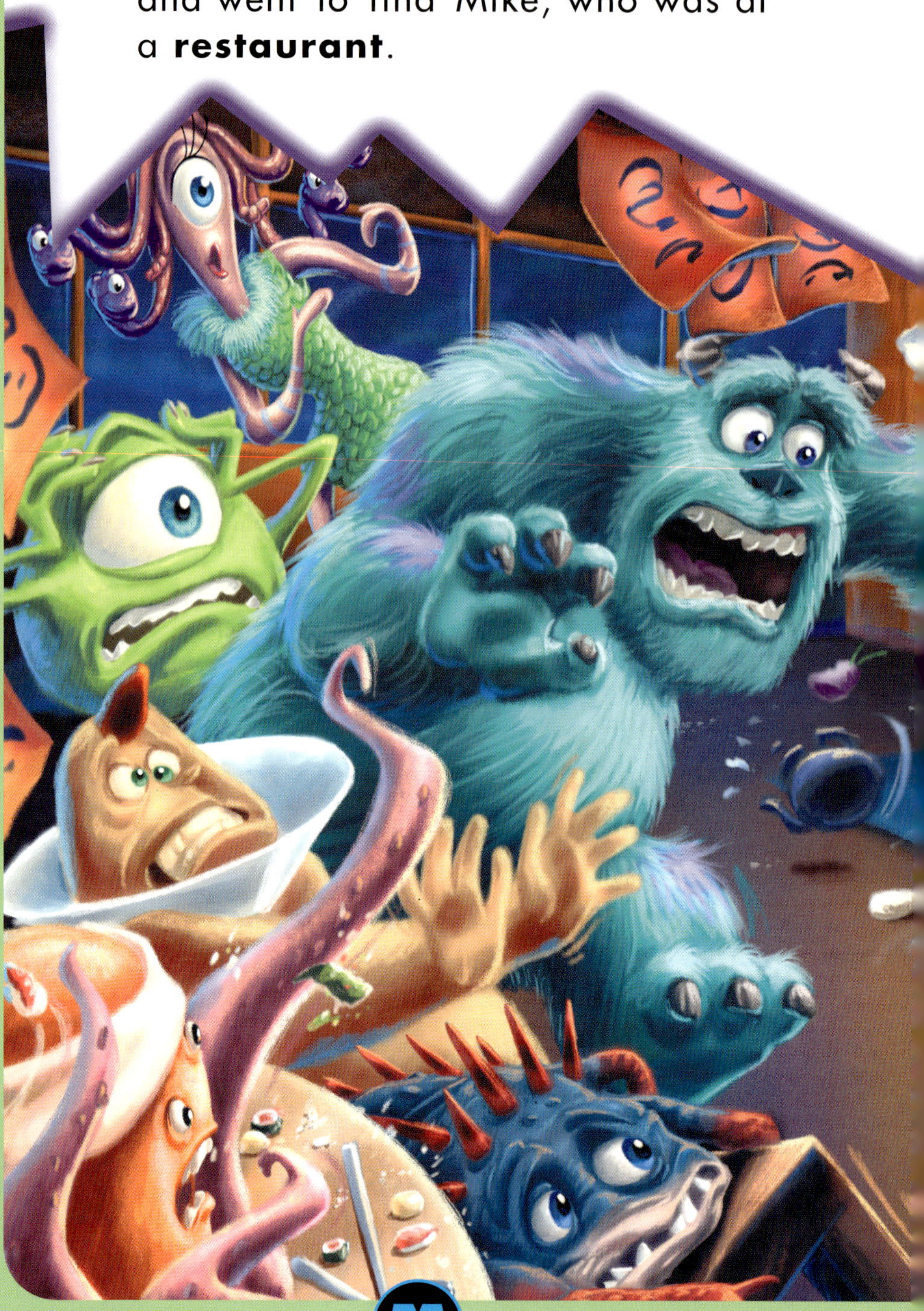

GO

STOP

Scarer

Suddenly, the little girl got out of the bag . . . and the monsters **hastily** got out of the restaurant!

If the other monsters **spied** her, she'd never get back to her room. So **swiftly** and **speedily**, Sulley and Mike **promptly** took her home.

For one night she stayed.
She giggled as she played.
The lights shone brighter from the laughter inside her.

Indeed, it seems that laughs are more powerful than screams.

"Boo!" she said.
So "Boo" is what Sulley called her.

The more Sulley cared for the little girl, the **crazier** it made Mike.

Boo went to sleep, **exhausted** from all the fun and laughter.

🗨️ Sulley knew he had to find Boo's **closet** door and take her home. To get her back into Monsters, Inc., Sulley and Mike had to make her look like a little monster.

Poor Boo!

Randall had other plans. He was in a **dangerous mood**, a **devious** mood, a chasing mood.

Oh no! Where, Sulley and Mike wondered, is Boo's **closet**?

Is it behind door number 1, door number 2, or door number 3–thousand?!

Would they find it before Randall found them?

GAME

RUSSIA

JAPAN

FRANCE

INDIA

SPAIN

GERMANY

CHINA

ITALY

U.S.A.

Scarer

Of course, **noble** Sulley and **courageous** Mike **outsmarted nasty** Randall...

...and brought Boo home at last. Safe in her own bed.

Sulley knew he'd found a friend.

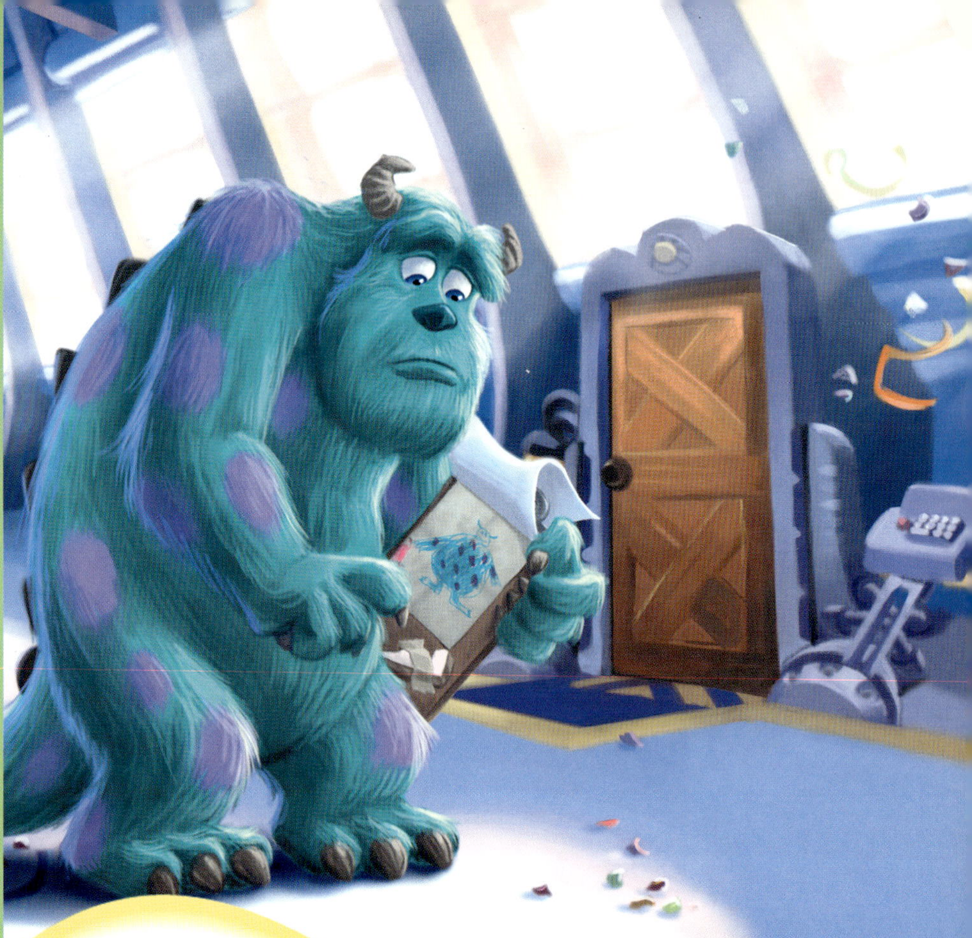

Sulley missed Boo.
Sulley was **sullen**.

But not for long! Every time he thought of Boo, he remembered her laughter and how her laughter made everything brighter, **including** the lights.

Laughter is more powerful than screams!

Scarer   Top Scarer

So the monsters at Monsters, Inc. listened to Sulley.
They stopped scaring children and began making them laugh!
**Giggle!
Chuckle!
Guffaw!**

More laughter? More **energy**!

And Boo?
Sulley went back and found her again.
They knew they would be
friends **forever**.

GAME

Trainee Scarer

MONSTERS, INC.   **FINAL EXAM**
WE SCARE BECAUSE WE CARE

Repeat

25

MONSTER HUNT

Welcome to the LeapPad™ Library!

LeapFrog® LEAP•START
Preschool-K • Up to Age 5

LEAP•START Books:
Reading Readiness and Simple Activities

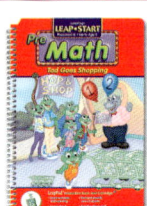 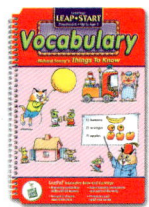 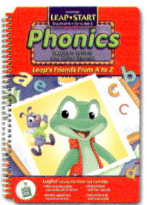 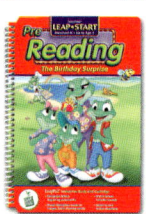

© 1991 Richard Scarry

LeapFrog® LEAP•1
Preschool-Grade 1 • Ages 4-6

LEAP•1 Books:
Learning to Read and Introduction to Simple Subjects

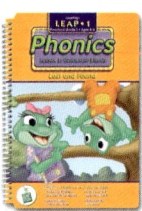 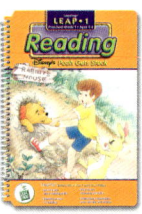 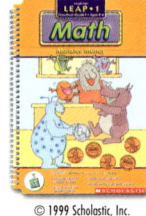 

© 1999 Disney Enterprises, Inc.   © 1999 Scholastic, Inc.

LeapFrog® LEAP•2
Grades 1-3 • Ages 6-8

LEAP•2 Books:
Reading Practice and School-Related Subjects

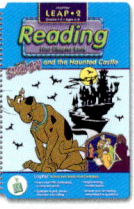 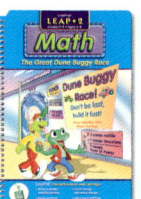 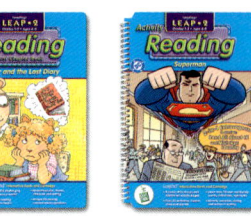

™ & © 1998 Hanna-Barbera   © 1998 Marc Brown   ™ & © 2001 DC Comics

LeapFrog® LEAP•3
Grades 3-5 • Ages 8-10

LEAP•3 Books:
Reading Comprehension and Reading to Learn

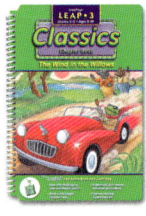 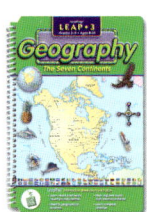 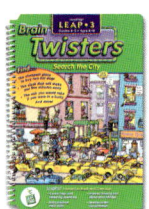 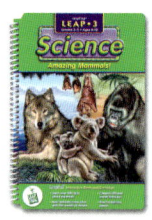

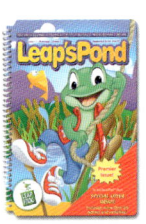

Join the LeapFrog® Never-Ending Learning Club for more learning fun for your *LeapPad* player.
Go to: www.leapfrog.com for information on how to join!